DoD 4100.39-M
Volume 7

FEDERAL LOGISTICS INFORMATION SYSTEM

FLIS PROCEDURES MANUAL

ESTABLISH/MAINTENANCE OF

ORGANIZATIONAL ENTITY AND

PROVISIONING SCREENING

MASTER ADDRESS TABLE

OCTOBER 2009

CHAPTER 1
ESTABLISHMENT/MAINTENANCE, CAGE CODE MASTER FILE (CAGE/NCAGE)

7.1.1 Introduction

a. The procedures in this chapter prescribe the input modes/formats and instructions to be followed by activities/agencies when submitting requests to the Defense Logistics Information Service (DLIS) for processing new code assignments and/or maintenance actions for:

(1) Commercial and Government Entity Code (CAGE). A five-position alphanumeric code with a numeric in the first and last positions (e.g., 27340, 2A345, 2AA45, or 2AAA5), excluding the letters I and O assigned to U.S. organizations which manufacture and/or control the design of items supplied to a Government Military or Civil Agency or assigned to U.S. organizations, primarily for identifying contractors in the mechanical interchange of data required by MILSCAP and the Service/Agency automatic data processing (ADP) systems. The CAGE data provides the data base for the LOLA and FEDLOG application and the H series products on CD-ROM.

(2) NATO Commercial and Government Entity (NCAGE) Code. A five position alphanumeric code requiring an alpha in either the first and/or fifth position excluding the letter O, (e.g., AA123, 3AAAA, 1234K, K2345 or A1234A), assigned to organizations located in North Atlantic Treaty Organization (NATO) member nations (excluding U.S.) and other foreign countries which manufacture and/or control the design of items supplied to a Government Military Activity or Civil Agency. The prefix (first position) of a NCAGE code of I, S, L, O, will not be utilized with any alpha suffix (fifth position) in the NCAGE Code structure.The NCAGE data provides the data base for the LOLA and FEDLOG application and the H series products on CD-ROM.

b. The FLIS design features of the DLIS CAGE Master CAGE/NCAGE File provide for submission of multi-media type input in a mechanized format. Resulting output from DLIS will be incorporated into the mechanized systems of recorded recipient Services and Agencies. (See volume 10, table 134 for DLIS/foreign governments responsible for assigning and maintaining CAGE/NCAGE).

c. Submission mode of proposed input transactions will be by an on-line system input by DLIS only.

d. Requests for new CAGE Codes will be submitted in one (1) of the following fashions:

(1) For Vendors not listed in the database, the CAGE request process is incorporated in the Central Contraction Registration (CCR). CCR is an authorized source for the assignment of CAGE Codes. CAGE Codes will be assigned to vendors as their CCR registration goes through the validation process.

(2) Vendors that require a CAGE Code for a Security Clearance or for the assignment of a DODAAC Code do not need to register in CCR. The request may be submitted on the DD Form 2051, "Request for Assignment of a Commercial and Government Entity (CAGE) Code." Section A must be filled out and signed

by the sponsoring government agency. The agency may also request the CAGE Code on their activity letterhead. (See Appendix 7-1-A).

(3) NATO Form AC/135-No. 2. This method is used when requesting NCAGE Codes for firms located outside the United States. A foreign company that performs work outside the United States is not required to register in CCR in order to be awarded a contract. Foreign registrants must have a NATO Commercial and Government Entity (NCAGE) Code assigned prior to registering in CCR. Companies shall be allowed to apply directly to the NATO Codification Bureau(s) NCBs for NCAGE Code assignments except in Italy, where national regulations prohibit this practice. For NCAGE assignments for companies located in Italy, you will need to make the request through the NCB of your country. You will find addresses and points of contact for Italy and other NATO NCBs at http://www.dlis.dla.mil/nato poc.asp. (See Appendix 7-1-B).

(4) Requests for maintenance actions received directly from companies not registered in CCR will continue to be processed by DLIS regardless of the media received.

(5) Letters and/or forms concerning the CAGE Code System will be directed to:

Commander
Defense Logistics Information Service
ATTN: DLIS-LAC
Federal Center
74 N. Washington, Suite 7
Battle Creek, MI 49017-3084

e. Prior to submission of a request for code assignment or maintenance action, activities/agencies will screen their files to ensure a CAGE/NCAGE has not already been assigned or updated for that particular organizational entity. DLIS sends out computer-generated letters to vendors registered in CCR requesting verification of the organization's status, making one complete cycle of the file annually. This factor should be considered; however, an activity/agency should not withhold information available concerning a CAGE Code because of this process.

f. The following references contain explicit instructions concerning formats and preparation of CAGE/NCAGE data to be forwarded to DLIS.

REFERENCE	CONTENT
Appendices 7-1-A and 7-1-B	Preparation of Forms
Volume 10	Multiple Application References/Instructions/Tables and Grids

g. Maintenance of FLIS Data Base. Following DLIS approval/processing of a transaction wherein a CAGE/NCAGE is cancelled and replaced by a CAGE/NCAGE involving one or more part numbers, a mass change of FLIS data base records will result from DLIS machine-generated LAR/LCR/LDR transactions. DLIS will provide the applicable activity/agency data receivers appropriate file maintenance data on KAR, and KCR transactions for updating their National Item Identification Number (NIIN) file records.

h. The CAGE Master File is the basis for the H series on CD-ROM product.

7.1.2 Add Total New Commercial and Government Entity or NATO Commercial and Government Entity Code

This section describes the criteria governing the assignment of new CAGE/NCAGE data, subsequently referred to as CAGE Type A - Manufacturers; Type E - NATO Manufacturers; and Type F - Non-manufacturers.

a. Add Total CAGE Record - Type A - CAGE Code.

(1) Activities/agencies will ensure that prior to submitting a request to DLIS for the assignment of a Type A new CAGE Code number that the code is in fact required for design documentation and/or operations pertaining to cataloging a new item or adding a new source of supply to an item already cataloged. In this regard, the code will be requested after the item has been procured from the new source and not before a solicitation has been made.

(2) The following kinds of organizations/functions are eligible for CAGE Code assignments:

(a) Manufacturing organizations that are the sources from which items of supply are obtained for use in the Federal Supply System.

(b) Commercial organizations that control the design of items used by the Federal Government but do not necessarily manufacture nor sell directly to the Government.

(c) Manufacturing organizations that produce items of industrial production equipment, and whose items are published in Industrial Plant Equipment Handbooks. (The manufacturer's code is published in conjunction with the Plant Equipment Codes assigned to the individual items of a given manufacturer.)

(d) Distributors who are sole sources of supply for items which cannot be purchased directly from the manufacturer located in the U.S., or any NATO member nation.

(e) Government agencies that manufacture items entering the Federal Supply or Military Industrial Systems, or control the design of such items without actually manufacturing them.

(f) Manufacturers who supply materials for incorporation into the products of contractors who provide drawings of these products to the Government under MIL-DTL-31000 or ASME-Y14.100; ASME-Y14.24; ASME-Y14.35m and ASME-Y14–34m.

(g) Manufacturers which require that a factory source code be "stamped or imprinted" in accordance with various military specifications/standards such as MIL-PRF-1 and MIL-STD-130K.

(h) Various kinds of Government specifications, and certain Government organizations connected with the development of standards and/or specifications.

(i) The CAGE Master File is the basis for H4, NATO Commercial and Government Entity (NCAGE) Code, LOLA and FEDLOG CAGE inquiry applications. Procedures governing LOLA Procedures are contained in volume 16 .

(3) Requests for new CAGE Code assignments to Government organizations or specifications and standards promulgated by Government organizations must be submitted on the letterhead of the agency/activity to which the code is to be assigned. They must specify the type of drawings, items, or documents controlled.

b. Add Total OE Record - Type F - CAGE Code.

(1) Submitting activities will ensure that the CAGE Code assignment is required for identifying an organization/function in MILSCAP, bid abstracts, purchase documents, and/or other documents pertaining to the contract/purchase agreement as required by DoD 40000.25-5-M MILSCAP Manual; Armed Services Procurement Regulation (ASPR); DoD Procurement Manual; and the DoD procurement circulars.

(2) The following kinds of organizations/functions are eligible for Type F CAGE Code assignments:

Manufacturing organizations not qualifying for a Type A CAGE Code.
Distributors.
Sales offices.
Retail establishments.
Service organizations.
Wholesale or jobbing establishments.
Professional organizations, including engineering.
Construction and mining firms.
Banks and universities.
Any other nongovernmental organizations which must be identified in MILSCAP data interchange.

c. Add Total CAGE Record - Type E - NCAGE.

(1) Only specific foreign codification authorities are presently empowered to assign NCAGEs to manufacturers or other organizational entities located in NATO and non-NATO countries (excluding U.S.).

(a) Foreign companies that perform work outside the U.S. are not required to register in CCR. Foreign registrants registering in CCR must have a NCAGE Code assigned prior to registration. If your orgainization does not already have an NCAGE Assigned, for most countries you can obtain one using the Form AC/135-No. 2 on the following http://www.dlis.dla.mil/Forms/Form AC135.asp.

(b) The requesting facility will submit to DLIS (ATTN: SBB) a completed DD Form 2051, Request for Assignment of CAGE Code/Contractor, accompanied by a letter of transmittal. The letter will enable DLIS to expedite confirmation of the NCAGE to the requester.

(c) If you cannot submit this form by Internet, you can obtain an NCAGE by contacting the National Codification Bureau of the country where your organization is located. For a list of addresses, go to http://www.dlis.dla.mil/nato poc.asp. Note to U.S.submitters: Organizations with an address containing APO, FPO, or AE do not need a NCAGE and should not fill out this form. Instead, register in the Central Contractor Registration (CCR) system at www.ccr.gov and you will receive a U.S. CAGE Code. Companies shall be allowed to apply directly to NCBs for NCAGE Code assignments except in Italy, where national regulations prohibit this practice. For NCAGE assignments for companies located in Italy, you will need to make the request through the NCB of your country. You will find addresses and points of contact for the Italy and other NATO NCBs at http:www.dlis.dla.mil/nato poc.asp. NATO National Codification Bureaus and other government offices may use the Internet Form 2 to request NCAGE assignments from Italy, and their name will be found in the drop down menu in Block 2 of the Form 2.

(2) The following kinds of non-NATO foreign organizations/functions are eligible for NCAGE assignments in connection with Federal supply cataloging operations:

(a) Manufacturers, distributors, or other entities that are the source from which items of supply are obtained for use in the Federal Supply System.

(b) Commercial organizations that control the design of items used by the Federal Government, but do not necessarily sell directly to the Government.

(c) Manufacturing organizations that produce items of industrial production equipment, and whose items are published in Industrial Plant Equipment Handbooks.(The manufacturer's code is published in conjunction with the Plant Equipment Codes assigned to the individual items of a given manufacturer.)

(d) Manufacturers who supply materials for incorporation into the products of contractors who provide drawings of these products to the Government under MIL-DTL-31000 or ASME-Y14.100; ASME-Y14.24; ASME-Y14.35m and ASME-Y14–34m.

(e) Manufacturers which require that a factory source code be "stamped or imprinted" in accordance with military specifications/standards such as MIL-PRF-1 and MIL-STD-130K.

7.1.3 Change Data to an Existing CAGE/NCAGE Record
This section describes the criteria for external requests to DLIS for adding, changing or deleting permissive data elements to an existing CAGE/NCAGE record.

a. Change Data to an Existing CAGE Record - Types A and F. Requests for maintenance actions will be submitted to DLIS on a DD Form 2051, correspondence prepared and signed by an official of the firm and from CCR.

b. Change data to an existing CAGE Record - Type E. DLIS will make the change solely at the direction of a specific foreign codification authority through the medium of correspondence and amendments or supplements.

7.1.4 Change-of-Name Agreements, Novation Agreements, Mergers and Sales of Assets
1. The contracting officer responsible for execution of a change-of-name agreement (see FAR Subpart 42.12) must submit the agreement of DLIS-LAC. If there are no current contracts, each contracting and contract

administration office receiving notification of changes from the commercial entity must forward a copy of the change notice annotated with the CAGE Code to DLIS-LAC unless the change notice indicates that DLIS-LAC already has been notified.

2. Contracting officers shall process and execute notation agreements in accordance with FAR Subpart 42.12, Notation and Change-of-Name Agreements. These actions are independent of code and name assignments made as a result of the occasion which created the need for the novation agreement. The maintenance activity will determine which entity(s) will retain the existing code(s) and which entities will be assigned new codes. The contracting officer responsible for processing the novation agreement shall provide the maintenance activity the following information:

    a. Name(s), address(es), and code(s) of the contractor(s) transferring the original contractual rights and obligations.

    b. Name(s), address(es), and code(s) (if any) of the entity who is the successor in interest (transferor).

    c. Name(s), address(es), and code(s) (if any) of the entity who is retaining or receiving the rights to the technical data.

    d. Description of the circumstances surrounding the novation agreement and especially the relationship of each entity to the other.

7.1.5 Cancel Total CAGE/NCAGE Code Record

This section describes the criteria for requesting a cancel CAGE transaction. These transactions will be used to change a CAGE status to cancel with or without replacement. They will not purge the record from the file in its entirety, but will purge such data as Post Office box number and street address. The only time a CAGE/NCAGE will be considered as a replacement for another code is when the succeeding firm has acquired all design, manufacturing, and/or patent rights to all product lines manufactured by the defunct organization and this fact is substantiated in writing by the firms involved. The fact that a firm manufacturers identical items, but did not acquire the rights of the defunct firm, does not qualify it as a replacement.

    a. Cancel Total CAGE Record - Type A - CAGE Code.

    (1) The information an activity/agency or company must submit to DLIS for evaluation purposes will include the following information as applicable:

    (a) Confirm that the coded facility has ceased all manufacturing operations. (In instances where a portion of the product lines have been discontinued or sold, a delete total CAGE Code transaction is not proper.)

    (b) If the coded facility has ceased all manufacturing operations in their entirety, determine if the operation was sold, including all design, manufacturing, and patent rights pertaining to items previously manufactured and furnished to the Government.

(c) If all manufacturing operations of a defunct firm have been sold (including all manufacturing, patent rights, etc.), advise whether such operations were acquired by a single successor firm or if multiple successor firms are involved.

(d) If all manufacturing operations of a defunct firm have been sold to a single successor firm, advise whether the successor firm has previously been assigned a CAGE Code.

(e) If all manufacturing operations of a defunct facility have been merged into one affiliated facility, advise whether the acquiring facility has previously been coded.

(2) If the proposed transaction does not include a replacement CAGE Code, the accompanying correspondence will contain just that information listed above which is necessary to ascertain that the organization is, in fact, defunct.

(3) If the proposed transaction does not include a replacement CAGE Code, the accompanying correspondence will provide the information listed in paragraph 7.1.4.a(1) necessary to ascertain that the replacement CAGE Code submitted is proper.

(4) If there is a known successor firm, but that firm is not coded, the pertinent information listed in paragraph 7.1.4.a(3) will be submitted to DLIS with the complete name and address of the successor organization. If, after evaluation, DLIS determines that a code should be obtained for the successor organization and a cancel/replace transaction submitted, such action will be taken by DLIS.

b. Cancel Total CAGE Record - Type F - CAGE Code. The information an activity/agency must submit to DLIS for evaluation purposes will include the following information as applicable:

(1) Indicate that the coded facility has ceased all operations, and is in fact defunct.

(2) If the coded facility has ceased all operations in its entirety, determine if the facility was sold.

(3) If the operations of a defunct firm have been sold to or merged with a single successor firm, determine if successor firm has previously been assigned a CAGE Code.

c. Cancel Total CAGE Record - Type E - NCAGE. A cancel Total CAGE transaction will be accomplished only by DLIS solely at the direction of a specific foreign codification authority through the medium of correspondence and amendments or supplements thereto. DLIS will prepare the documents.

7.1.6 Reinstate Cancelled CAGE/NCAGE Record

This section describes the criteria for external requests to DLIS for reinstating CAGE records that are recorded on the DLIS CAGE Master File as cancelled.

a.Reinstate Cancelled CAGE Record - Types A and F. Requests for reinstatement actions will be submitted to DLIS on a DD Form 2051 or correspondence prepared by an official of the firm.

b. Reinstate Cancelled CAGE Code Record - Type E. DLIS will make the change solely at the direction of a specific foreign codification authority through the medium of correspondence.

7.1.7 Outputs from Processing CAGE Code Master File Records

This section encompasses the output data distribution system employed by DLIS. Specific data receivers of CAGE file maintenance data are determined by each requiring Service/Agency. Output mode(s) for dissemination of data is predicated on the specific type of output transaction, data involved, and activity/agency mode of communication for receiving data from DLIS; i.e., electronic data transmission (message data), magnetic tape, correspondence, FAX, and telephone.

a. NIIN File Maintenance Update. Following approval/processing of a Total OE input transaction containing a replacement CAGE code number involving one or more FLIS part numbers, DLIS will provide the applicable activity/agency receivers with appropriate FLIS file maintenance data for updating their NIIN file records. Update actions for deletion of a cancelled CAGE code and adding of a replacement CAGE code are accomplished by DLIS forwarding machine-generated KDR, KCR, and KAR transactions to data receivers.

b. CAGE SSR File Maintenance Service (DIC KHN). Provides activities/agencies machine sensitive records to establish and maintain a CAGE file containing each assigned CAGE/NCAGE related data as recorded and maintained on the DLIS Master Consolidated CAGE/NCAGE File. This service is available only to recipients of the basic file. (See volume 8, chapter 8.2 for format.)

(1) CAGE data includes Type CAGE Code, CAGE Code number, company names, street address, city, state/country, Foreign/Domestic Designator, CAGE Replacement Code, CAGE Status Code, CAGE Designator Code, ZIP Code, Contract Administration Office (CAO), and Automatic Data Processing (ADP) Point (as applicable), and related socioeconomic data.

(a) The Status Code designates a specific status condition related to a CAGE Code. There may be two complete records for a CAGE code; however, only one record is shown in a current status. (See volume 10, table 19)

(b) The complete package for each CAGE/NCAGE consists of one or more records. Each record will be 80 positions in length.

(2) Requests for CAGE Master file maintenance service will be processed through normal headquarters office channels. This will permit the release of the latest information available.

(3) File maintenance is available by means of electronic data transmission (for telecommunications procedures controlling electronic transmission see volume 2, paragraph 2.3.2.d). Data records will be released on a daily basis.

c. The basic CAGE Master File will be provided to agencies/activities on magnetic tape upon receipt of their written requirements, forwarded through their appropriate command headquarters. The basic file will be contained on two reels of magnetic tape, provided by DLIS, and forwarded to the requesting activity by certified mail. Format will be in accordance with DIC KHN, volume 8, chapter 8.2 .

(1) The basic file will contain OE File Maintenance Transaction Code 003 data only.

(2) DLIS has the capability of providing tapes with any of the characteristics described in volume 10, table 10 .

d. The normal mode of output for CAGE will be electronic data transmission when the activity possesses electronic receiving capabilities.

e. For those activities/agencies that do not possess electronic capabilities internet access is available, except when CAGE Codes are assigned to U.S. firms for a NATO government. Then confirmation will be on NATO Form AC/135-NR.2, section B. (See appendix 7-1-B)

CHAPTER 1
APPENDIX 7-1-A
PREPARATION of DD FORM 2051

Requests for assignment of new CAGE Codes must be submitted through CCR, unless the code is required to support security clearances or DODAAC Code assignment. These requests will be submitted on the DD Form 2051, "Request for Assignment of a Commercial and Government Entity (CAGE) Code." Section A must be filled out and signed by a sponsoring government agent. The requesting agency is responsible for assuring that the DD Form 2051 is properly completed and forwarded to DLIS. The agency may also request the CAGE Code on their agency letterhead.

Following are examples of completed DD Forms 2051 for code assignment and a request for an update to a previously assigned code.

The third illustration of this appendix reflects DD Form 2051 instructions as they appear on the reverse of the form.

Please note the address on the back of DD Form 2051 should read:
Commander
Defense Logistics Information Service
ATTN: DLIS-LAC
Hart-Dole-Inouye Federal Center
74 North Washington
Battle Creek, MI 49017-3084

REQUEST FOR ASSIGNMENT OF A COMMERCIAL AND GOVERNMENT ENTITY (CAGE) CODE
(See Instructions on back)

Form Approved
OMB No. 0704-0226
Expires Aug 31, 2001

The public reporting burden for this collection of information is estimated to average 7 minutes per response, including the time for reviewing instructions, searching existing data sources, gathering and maintaining the data needed, and completing and reviewing the collection of information. Send comments regarding this burden estimate or any other aspect of this collection of information, including suggestions for reducing the burden, to Department of Defense, Washington Headquarters Services, Directorate for Information Operations and Reports (0704-0226), 1215 Jefferson Davis Highway, Suite 1204, Arlington, VA 22202-4302. Respondents should be aware that notwithstanding any other provision of law, no person shall be subject to any penalty for failing to comply with a collection of information if it does not display a currently valid OMB control number.

PLEASE DO NOT RETURN YOUR FORM TO THIS ADDRESS. SEND COMPLETED FORM TO ADDRESS ON BACK.

SECTION A - TO BE COMPLETED BY INITIATOR

1. REQUESTING GOVERNMENT AGENCY/ACTIVITY

a. NAME: DESC (728)

b. ADDRESS

STREET

2. TYPE CODE REQUESTED (X one)	3. EXCEPTION CODES		CITY	STATE	ZIP CODE
a. TYPE A	a. CAO	NA	Dayton	OH	43215
b. TYPE F	b. AOP	NA			

4. INITIATOR

a. TYPED NAME (Last, First, Middle Initial)	b. OFFICE SYMBOL	c. SIGNATURE	d. TELEPHONE NO. (Include area code)
SMITH, JANE L.	DESC-SC		DSN 850-6129

SECTION B - TO BE COMPLETED BY FIRM TO BE CODED

5. FIRM

a. NAME (Include Branch of, Division of, etc.): ABC ELECTRONICS, INC

b. ADDRESS
STREET: 123 S. 2nd Street

c. CAGE CODE (If previously assigned)

CITY	STATE	ZIP CODE
Dayton	OH	45444

6. IF FIRM PREVIOUSLY OPERATED UNDER OTHER NAME(S) OR OTHER ADDRESS(ES) SPECIFY THE PREVIOUS NAME(S) AND/OR ADDRESS(ES) (Use separate sheet of paper, if necessary)

NA

7. PARENT COMPANY AND AFFILIATED FIRMS (X one, and complete as applicable)

X a. NONE

b. CURRENTLY AFFILIATED WITH OTHER FIRMS (List name(s) and address(es) of such firms on a separate sheet of paper)

c. PREVIOUSLY AFFILIATED WITH OTHER FIRMS (List name(s) and address(es) of such firms on a separate sheet of paper)

8. PRIMARY BUSINESS CATEGORY (X one)

X a. MANUFACTURER
b. DEALER/DISTRIBUTOR
c. CONSTRUCTION FIRM
d. SERVICE COMPANY
e. SALES OFFICE
f. OTHER (Specify)

9. SMALL DISADVANTAGED BUSINESS STATUS (X one)

a. APPROVED BY SMALL BUSINESS ADMINISTRATION (SBA) FOR SECTION 8(a) PROGRAM
b. OTHER SMALL DISADVANTAGED BUSINESS CONCERN
c. NOT SMALL DISADVANTAGED BUSINESS CONCERN

10. NUMBER OF EMPLOYEES 57

11. WOMEN-OWNED BUSINESS CONCERN (X one) [X] a. YES [ ] b. NO

12. NORTH AMERICAN INDUSTRY CLASSIFICATION SYSTEM (NAICS) CODES
a. PRIMARY 3615
b. OTHER (Specify)

13. REMARKS

FOR ASSIGNMENT OF A SECURITY CLEARANCE

FOR ASSIGNMENT OF A DODAAC CODE

14. FIRM OFFICIAL

a. TYPED NAME (Last, First, Middle Initial)	b. DATE SIGNED (YYYYMMDD)	c. SIGNATURE	d. TELEPHONE NO. (Include area code)
CHARLIE, ABLE B	20030130		513-212-6712

DD FORM 2051, NOV 2000   PREVIOUS EDITION IS OBSOLETE.

REQUEST FOR ASSIGNMENT OF A COMMERCIAL AND GOVERNMENT ENTITY (CAGE) CODE
(See instructions on back.)

Form Approved
OMB No. 0704-0226
Expires Aug 31, 2001

The public reporting burden for this collection of information is estimated to average 7 minutes per response, including the time for reviewing instructions, searching existing data sources, gathering and maintaining the data needed, and completing and reviewing the collection of information. Send comments regarding this burden estimate or any other aspect of this collection of information, including suggestions for reducing the burden, to Department of Defense, Washington Headquarters Services, Directorate for Information Operations and Reports (0704-0226), 1215 Jefferson Davis Highway, Suite 1204, Arlington, VA 22202-4302. Respondents should be aware that notwithstanding any other provision of law, no person shall be subject to any penalty for failing to comply with a collection of information if it does not display a currently valid OMB control number.
PLEASE DO NOT RETURN YOUR FORM TO THIS ADDRESS. SEND COMPLETED FORM TO ADDRESS ON BACK.

SECTION A - TO BE COMPLETED BY INITIATOR

1. REQUESTING GOVERNMENT AGENCY/ACTIVITY

a. NAME	b. ADDRESS
DSCC	STREET

2. TYPE CODE REQUESTED (X one)	3. EXCEPTION CODES	CITY	STATE	ZIP CODE
X a. TYPE A	a. CAO	Columbus	OH	43215
b. TYPE F	b. ADP			

4. INITIATOR

a. TYPED NAME (Last, First, Middle Initial)	b. OFFICE SYMBOL	c. SIGNATURE	d. TELEPHONE NO. (include area code)
CUTE, I. M	DSCC-SC		DSN 850-7721

SECTION B - TO BE COMPLETED BY FIRM TO BE CODED

5. FIRM

a. NAME (Include Branch of, Division of, etc.)	b. ADDRESS
Jones and Smith, Incorporated	STREET 640 S. Borad Street

c. CAGE CODE (If previously assigned)	CITY	STATE	ZIP CODE
1ABC6	Columbus	OH	43215

6. IF FIRM PREVIOUSLY OPERATED UNDER OTHER NAME(S) OR OTHER ADDRESS(ES) SPECIFY THE PREVIOUS NAME(S) AND/OR ADDRESS(ES) (Use separate sheet of paper, if necessary.)	7. PARENT COMPANY AND AFFILIATED FIRMS (X one, and complete as applicable)
Jones Machine Shop 619 S. 12th Street Columbus, OH 43215	X a. NONE
	b. CURRENTLY AFFILIATED WITH OTHER FIRMS (List name(s) and address(es) of such firms on a separate sheet of paper)
	c. PREVIOUSLY AFFILIATED WITH OTHER FIRMS (List name(s) and address(es) of such firms on a separate sheet of paper)

8. PRIMARY BUSINESS CATEGORY (X one)	9. SMALL DISADVANTAGED BUSINESS STATUS (X one)	10. NUMBER OF EMPLOYEES 99
a. MANUFACTURER	a. APPROVED BY SMALL BUSINESS ADMINIS- TRATION (SBA) FOR SECTION 8(a) PROGRAM	11. WOMEN-OWNED BUSINESS CONCERN (X one) ☐ a. YES ☒ b. NO
b. DEALER/DISTRIBUTOR		
X c. CONSTRUCTION FIRM		
d. SERVICE COMPANY	b. OTHER SMALL DISADVANTAGED BUSINESS CONCERN	12. NORTH AMERICAN INDUSTRY CLASSI- FICATION SYSTEM (NAICS) CODES
e. SALES OFFICE		a. PRIMARY 3712
f. OTHER (Specify)	c. NOT SMALL DISADVANTAGED BUSINESS CONCERN	b. OTHER (Specify)

13. REMARKS

FOR ASSIGNMENT OF A SECURITY CLEARANCE

FOR ASSIGNMENT OF A DODAAC CODE

14. FIRM OFFICIAL

a. TYPED NAME (Last, First, Middle Initial)	b. DATE SIGNED (YYYYMMDD)	c. SIGNATURE	d. TELEPHONE NO. (include area code)
U. R. NICE	20030129		999-999-9999

DD FORM 2051, NOV 2000   PREVIOUS EDITION IS OBSOLETE.

INSTRUCTIONS FOR COMPLETING DD FORM 2051

GENERAL NOTE FOR PERSONNEL PREPARING OR PROCESSING THIS REPORT

Coding must be as indicated in the instructions. Noncompliance with the coding instructions contained herein will make the organization that fails to comply responsible for required concessions in data base communication.

SPECIFIC INSTRUCTIONS

SECTION A - TO BE COMPLETED BY THE INITIATING GOVERNMENT ACTIVITY

Item 1. Self-explanatory.

Item 2. Mark the type of code being requested.

a. Type A - Manufacturers Code, which is used in the Federal Catalog System to identify a certain facility at a specific location that is a possible source for the manufacture and/or design control of items cataloged by the Federal Government; or,

b. Type F - Non-manufacturers Code, which is required for identifying an organization/function in MILSCAP. These are assigned to contractors that are non-manufacturers or that are manufacturers not qualifying for a Type A Code.

Item 3. If applicable, enter the exception DoD Activity Address Code for the Servicing Contract Administration Office (CAO) or ADP point.

Item 4. Self-explanatory.

SECTION B - TO BE COMPLETED BY THE FIRM TO WHICH THE CODE WILL BE ASSIGNED

Item 5.a. and b. Self explanatory.

c. If a CAGE Code (Type A or Type F) was previously assigned, enter it in this block.

Item 6. Self explanatory.

Item 7. If a block other than "None" is marked, identify the Parent company by a (P) beside the firm name.

Item 8. Self explanatory.

SECTION B - (Continued)

Item 9. A small disadvantaged business concern is defined in Section 19.001 of the Federal Acquisition Regulation.

Item 10. Enter the number of employees. This number should include the employees of all affiliates.

Item 11. A women-owned business concern is defined in Section 52.204-5 of the Federal Acquisition Regulation.

Item 12. The NAICS Code is a Government Index that is used to identify business activity and that indicates the function (manufacturer, wholesaler, retailer, or service) and the line of business in which the company is engaged. If multiple NAICS Codes apply, indicate the primary first, then next important, etc.

Item 13. Self-explanatory.

Item 14. Self-explanatory.

NOTE: When any future changes are made to the coded facility (e.g. name change, location change, business sold, or operations discontinued), written notification stating the appropriate change should be sent to:

Commander
Defense Logistics Services Center
ATTN: DLSC SBB
Federal Center
74 North Washington
Battle Creek, MI 49017-3084

CHAPTER 1
APPENDIX 7-1-B
PREPARATION of NATO FORM AC/135-NR-2

When North Atlantic Treaty Organization governments require assignment of CAGE Codes for firms located in the United States, NATO Form AC/135-NR-2 will be submitted with the A portion completed as shown in the following example. DLIS will complete the B portion as shown and return to the requesting Agency.

Part A

Block	Instructions
1	Indicate the code of the requesting NCB or NAMSA (e.g. ZX).
2	Indicate date and the national reference (optional).
3	Indicate the code of the assigning NCB (e.g. YB).
4	Checkmark the appropriate box.
5	Checkmark the appropriate box.
6	The maximum information must be transmitted: the exact name, the geographical and/or postal address and the telephone must be stated. Any known abbreviations of the name of the firm/organization are also to be indicated. If the name includes "Department of", "Division of" "Branch of", etc. of a parent company, include this as part of the address. The requesting country will assume that the "manufacturer" or "organization" meets the definition given in Sub-Section 241.
8	The Government Contract Number (e.g. MIL-D-70237) and/or any other purpose as the materiel to be identified should be stated. List at least two typical identifying sets of numbers, letters or other symbols furnished by the manufacturer/organization to be coded and state name(s) of the item(s).
9	Any information available about known production should be given in order to facilitate the work of assigning Bureau. The offical address of the head office, as well as the address of the factory actually producing the items in question, should be given here.
10	Signature of the responsible authority.

NATO CODIFICATION SYSTEM - SYSTEME OTAN DE CODIFICATION

REQUEST FOR A NATO COMMERCIAL AND GOVERNMENT ENTITY CODE (NCAGE) / DEMANDE D'UN CODE ORGANISME COMMERCIAL OU GOUVERNEMENTAL OTAN (NCAGE)

PART A

1	FROM / DE	3	TO / POUR

2	REFERENCE : DATE

4	REQUESTED NCAGE CODE FOR / CODE NCAGE DEMANDE

☐ Manufacturer / Fabricant ☐ Vendor / Distributeur ☐ NATO or International Organisation / Organisation OTAN ou Internationale ☐ Provider of Services / Fournisseur de Services

5	PRIORITY / PRIORITE

☐ Emergency / Urgente ☐ Accelerated / Accélérée ☐ Routine / Routine

6	NAME AND ADDRESS / NOM ET ADRESSE
NA1	Manufacturer Name / Nom de Fabricant
ST1	Street / Rue
POB	P.O. Box / Boîte Postale
CIT	City / Ville
STE	State or Province (US and Canada only) / Etat ou Province (seulement EU et Canada)
STT	State or Province (other than US and Canada) / Etat ou Province (autres que EU et Canada)
CTR	Country / Pays
PCC	Postal City / Ville Postale
PSC	Postal Code / Code Postal
PCS	POB Postal Code / Code Postal BP
TEL	Tel. No./ N° Tél
TLX	Telex No./ N° Telex
FAX	Fax No./ N° Télécopieur
VTX	Videotex No./ N° Vidéotex
BOX	Telebox No./ N° Courrier Electronique
PSS	Packet Switched Service No. / N° Réseau Commuté de Paquets
INF	Internal National Information / Information Nationale Interne

7	FORMER NAME AND NCAGE CODE / ANCIENS NOM ET CODE NCAGE

8	TYPICAL REFERENCE NUMBERS / NUMEROS DE REFERENCE TYPIQUES

9	REMARKS / REMARQUES	10	SIGNATURE

NATO FORM AC/135 No. 2   FORMULAIRE OTAN AC/135 N° 2

NATO CODIFICATION SYSTEM - SYSTEME OTAN DE CODIFICATION

REQUEST FOR A NATO COMMERCIAL AND GOVERNMENT ENTITY CODE (NCAGE) / DEMANDE D'UN CODE ORGANISME COMMERCIAL OU GOUVERNEMENTAL OTAN (NCAGE)

PART B

1	FROM / DE	3	TO / POUR

2	REFERENCE : DATE

4	ASSIGNED NCAGE CODE / CODE NCAGE ATTRIBUE	5	REVISED NAME AND ADDRESS AS INDICATED / NOM ET ADRESSE REVISES COMME INDIQUE

6	REMARKS / REMARQUES	7	SIGNATURE

NATO FORM AC/135 No. 2   FORMULAIRE OTAN AC/135 N° 2

CHAPTER 2
ESTABLISHMENT/MAINTENANCE OF PROVISIONING SCREENING MASTER ADDRESS TABLE (PSMAT)

7.2.1 Registration in the PSMAT

a. These instructions cover the procedures to be used to register activities as users of the Defense Logistics Information Service provisioning screening services and to record such activities and their requirements in the DLIS Provisioning Screening Master Address Table. (See volume 10, table 23)

b. 1-2 days prior to the initial submittal of LSF or LSR search transactions, the submitters and receivers requirements and address data must be registered in the PSMAT under an applicable Destination Code, Screening. Only a Government Service or Agency is authorized to establish and maintain registrations in the PSMAT. Non-Government activities (private sector) must submit their requests through the authorizing Government agency or Service activity. DLIS-L will advise the submitter as soon as the registration is effected. If the submitter does not receive such notification, a follow-up inquiry will be made prior to the submission of screening requests.

c. A letter of registration is required as the authorization for activities and their contractors to participate in the DLIS provisioning screening program and to provide for their registration in the DLIS PSMAT. The letter of registration must be submitted to DLIS by the responsible Government activity and will contain the following information:

Type of input (establish, change, delete)
Recipients complete mailing address(es)
Media of output (see volume 10, table 10)
Alternate media of output (electronic data transfer) (see volume 10, table 10)
Activity Code, Screening (DRN 0177)
Destination Code, Screening (DRN 3890)
Service Code (see volume 10, table 42)
Communications Routing Indicator Code (electronic data)
Authorization for Catalog Management Data (CMD)

Submitters who require the return of provisioning screening results by mail will submit a letter of registration. (See appendix 7-2-B) and Submitters who will receive provisioning screening results electronically will establish their registration through the submission of a letter of registration. (See appendix 7-2-A).

The letter of registration may be forwarded either by E-mail to DLIS-LF contact at prvsngscrng@dlis.dla.mil or will be addressed to:

Commander

Defense Logistics Information Service
ATTN: DLIS-L (Provisioning Screening)
Federal Center
74 Washington Ave N.
Battle Creek, MI 49037-3084

d. Notification to Contractors. When a contractor is to be established as a registrant in the DLIS PSMAT, the responsible Government activity will furnish the contractor the destination and the activity codes prior to the preparation of provisioning screening requests by the contractor. This will be done no later than 15 days after the receipt of a request for these codes from the contractor.

e. Multiple Addressees. When multiple output of screening results is requested, all addressees registered under the applicable destination code will receive the results of screening. When single output is requested, only the first addressee in the register (under the applicable destination code) will receive the results.

7.2.2 Maintenance of the DLIS Master Address Table

It will be the responsibility of the Government activity having cognizance of the screening requirements of the contractors to update and purge the PSMAT according to current requirements. However; if it becomes apparent that the PSMAT address(es) requires an update, DLIS-LF will contact the service agency and/or contractor. If the contact is unsuccessful, then DLIS-LF will have the authority to delete the address(es) from the PSMAT. Special attention should be directed to deletion of addresses and destination codes upon completion of contractual obligations or Service/Agency requirements.

7.2.3 Required Information

a. Type of Input

Establish. Input used to establish a new destination code and related address information, or to add a new recipient's address information to an existing destination code in the DLIS Master Address Table.

Change. Input used to change address information or output media in an existing address and destination code.

Delete. Input used to delete a destination code and all related address information or delete an address from a destination code.

b. Activity Code, Screening (DRN 0177). The two-position code designating the submitter or responsible Government activity (as listed in, but not restricted to, volume 10, table 104; e.g., TG Warner Robins AFB, KE Aviation Supply Office, etc.).

c. Destination Code, Screening (DRN 3890). The five-position code which identifies the recipient(s) of provisioning screening results. It may be any combination of alphanumerics as designated by the submitter. For a government activity submitter, it must contain at least two alpha characters in order to preclude duplication of a valid CAGE/NCAGE. The destination code for a contractor may consist of, but is not restricted to its assigned CAGE/NCAGE.

d. Service Code, Provisioning Screening Destination Table (DRN 0264). A two-position numeric code designating the Military Service component or Civil Agency authorizing the submission of provisioning screening requests. Used internally by DLIS only for statistical purposes. (See volume 10, table 42 .)

e. Output Mode/Media Code (DRN 3740). A two-position alphanumeric code which designates the mode and media by which the output data is desired by the recipients of provisioning screening results. (see Appendix 1, Table 10, Output Mode/Media Code)

f. Alternate Media of Output Code (DRN 3740). The output mode and media code in this position designates the alternate mode and media of output desired when the results of screening exceed electronic data output limitation (See DIC KEC) or when there is a degradation of electronic transmission. (See volume 10, table 23 , note 3.)

g. Provisioning Screening Receiver's Address (DRN 0232). The multiple line information in the exact format required to mail the output product to the recipient(s) of provisioning screening data. A separate line will be used for each line of address information as set forth in the previous instruction. An attention line if used, should be placed before the street and city address information and should be an office symbol, room number, etc. A person's name should not be used unless absolutely necessary.

h. CMD Authorization Code (DRN 0759). A one-position numeric code which indicates whether or not a recipient is authorized to receive Catalog Management Data. Code 1 indicates the recipient is authorized, Code 2 indicates he is not.

CHAPTER 2
APPENDIX 7-2-A
SAMPLE LETTER OF REGISTRATION (ELECTRONIC DATA TRANSMISSION USERS)

XXXXXXXXXX   XXXXXXXXXX

                                                     XXXXXXXXXXX

XXXXXXXXXXX

Commander
Defense Logistics Information Service
Directorate of Logistics Information Management
ATTN: DLIS-L (Provisioning and Other Preprocurement Screening)
Federal Center
Battle Creek, MI 49037-3084

SUBJECT: Request for Registration as an Electronic Data Recipient of Provisioning and Other Preprocurement Screening Results

   Following information pertinent to registration as an electronic data recipient of results of provisioning and other preprocurement screening is being furnished in accordance with volume 7, paragraph 7.2.1.c , DoD 4100.39-M.

   Input (Establish, Change, Delete)
   Activity Code - TG
   Destination Code - 12345
   Service Code - 03
   Media of Data - M2 (Fixed Length Record Format Record)
   Alternate Media of Ouput - C2 (Cartridge Tape)
   Address Information

Communication Routing Indicator Code - XX (per JANAP 128) XX

This contractor is/is not authorized to receive Catalog Management Data (CMD).

   (signed)

SAMPLE LETTER OF REGISTRATION (EXCEPT ELECTRONIC DATA TRANSMISSION USERS)

XXXXXXXXXX   XXXXXXXXXX

XXXXXXXXXX   XXXXXXXXXX

Commander
Defense Logistics Information Service
Directorate of Logistics Information Management
ATTN: DLIS-L (Provisioning Screening)
Federal Center
Battle Creek, MI 49037-3084

SUBJECT: Request for Registration as Recipient of Provisioning and Other Preprocurement Screening Results

The following information is furnished pursuant to the above subject request:

Input (Establish, Change, Delete)
Activity Code - TG
Destination Code - 12345
Service Code - 03
Output Media Code - P7
Alternate Media of Output - P7
Point of Contact:
Telephone Number:
FAX Number:
Address Information

This contractor is/is not authorized to receive Catalog Management Data (CMD).

(signed)